A Father's Thoughts on Living

Walter D. Smith

Also by Walter D. Smith

Soar With the Eagles:
Principles, Practices, and Insightful Stories
to Help You Achieve Your Hopes and Dreams

A Father's Thoughts on Living

Walter D. Smith

Change Your Life Books
Mailing Address: P. O. Box 287
Rescue, California 95672

A Father's Thoughts on Living

Copyright © 2000 by Walter D. Smith

Published in paperback in 2000 by:  Change Your Life Books
P. O. Box 287
Rescue, California 95672
cylbooks@aol.com

All rights reserved. No part of this book may be reproduced in any form or by any electronic or mechanical means, including information storage and retrieval systems, without permission in writing from the publisher, except by a reviewer who may quote brief passages in a review.

Cover design: Ad Graphics, Inc., Tulsa, Oklahoma
Cover photo: Darton Drake
Printed in the United States of America

First Edition

ISBN: 0-9669032-8-5

A Father's Thoughts on Living

Although my life has been very blessed, the balance between my family and work has suffered. Many times I was away from home for extended periods, and as a result, I missed important years of my six children's lives.

My children, now grown and some with families of their own, grew up not knowing much about me, my parents and family, or my attitudes, philosophies, and other intangibles that make up who I am and guide what I do.

One day, I began to write down thoughts inspired by conversations, observations, and moments of reflection. All of

which shaped my philosophies and helped shape my life. Before I knew it, a collection of several hundred random thoughts had accumulated which I began to share with my children.

By sharing those thoughts with my children, I hoped to provide them with some insight into their father's ideas and beliefs. I also felt it was an opportunity to positively influence them, stimulate their thoughts, and help develop and reinforce their own philosophies.

My wishes for you are the same. May God be as kind to you as He has been to me, and may He bless you with a happy, healthy, rewarding, and productive life.

Walter D. Smith

*For my wife, children, and grandchildren
who provide endless inspiration and
whose love and support sustain me.*

TABLE OF CONTENTS

ACKNOWLEDGMENTS xii
PROLOGUE xiv

Random Thoughts to Get You Started 1
Be All That You Can Be 5
…and to the Republic for which it stands. 8
Show Me Don't Tell Me 11
Lend a Helping Hand 12
Time in a Bottle 15
In God We Trust 19

A Father's Thoughts on Living

Family Tradition	24
Never Too Old to Learn	26
Oh Happy Day	27
The Color of Money	30
Use It or Lose It	32
Tomorrow's Leaders	38
Love Conquers All	42
Right and Wrong	45
Half Full or Half Empty?	48
Go the Extra Mile	51
Take a Chance	60
When You Dream	61
Word Power	63
Compassion	68

Walter D. Smith

Teamwork	72
Differences of Opinion	74
Random Thoughts to Keep You Going	79
Leader of the Pack	82
Make 'em Laugh	86
Lessons Learned	88
False Impressions	92
Self Control	93
Personal Growth: Work in Progress	96
Uncertainty	104
Knowledge is Power	105
Health and Well Being	107
You're Only Human	108
Friendship	110

The Road to Ruin	113
Give	119
Lasting Impressions	121
To Tell the Truth	122
Make the Most of It	124
Take Note	126
Believe in Yourself	127
Making Decisions and Taking Action	130
If You Do the Job, Do it Right!	131
Forward March	133
Random Thoughts to Wrap Things Up	135

EPILOGUE 139

ACKNOWLEDGMENTS

The dedicated efforts of Annie Engelhardt and Derek Smith were instrumental in the production of this book.

Annie, a long time associate, had the unenviable task of transcribing my handwritten notes, which she, as always, did with remarkable efficiency and accuracy.

Derek, my son, is not only responsible for organizing and editing my thoughts but also for the layout. His professionalism and attention to detail greatly enhanced the book's quality.

I was blessed with the services and commitment of those two individuals to whom I owe a tremendous debt of gratitude. Thank you both.

In addition, I am grateful for the professional services of *Change Your Life Publishing Company* and *Ad Graphics* in the persons of Lou Ann Smith, Jim Weems and Barbara Weems who collaborated on layout, final editing and cover design.

Photographs were taken by Master Photographer Darton Drake who has been a great resource on several projects.

W.D.S.

PROLOGUE

I am lucky and blessed. I was born during the Great Depression and raised during World War II. I served in Korea shortly after the Korean War. I traveled Europe and Africa and observed extreme hunger and poverty. I worked with many people in many job capacities and industries throughout the world.

I have seen America rise from the depths of the Depression. I have witnessed the American people band together and rally around the American flag to defeat oppressive foreign governments. I have seen great advances in medicine, science, and technology.

I have been able to participate in the American Dream. I have grown from a child whose family owned nothing to a man who longs for nothing material.

Could my life have been so varied and rich at any other time in history or in any other country? I doubt it. America is truly the Land of the Free and the Home of the Brave. I love her with all my heart and soul.

Though I have heard and sung it a thousand times, I still get shivers up and down my spine and tears in my eyes when "The Star Spangled Banner" is played. God bless America and keep her free – a beacon of hope to the rest of the world.

Walter D. Smith

A Father's Thoughts on Living

Random Thoughts to Get You Started

Look hard and dig deep, and you will find some good in everyone.

Encourage.

Good deeds shout and get attention, but words are often ignored.

Walter D. Smith

All the weasels are not in the animal kingdom.

The eyes of a person reveal a lot.

Humans are motivated by pride, profit, pleasure, and protection. Learn this lesson early in life and teach it to your children.

Ambition pursued with a plan for service is admirable, but blind ambition has little merit.

A Father's Thoughts on Living

Don't let the lives of your loved ones pass you by.

Happiness is frequently in short supply, but there always seems to be enough misery to go around.

It is better to give than to receive, but it seems to be tougher and tougher for the givers to keep pace with the takers, because not all takers are needy.
Some are just lazy and dishonest.

Walter D. Smith

Know the distinction between being smart and being a smart aleck.

A gift given begrudgingly is a flawed gift.

Scorn and rejection fuel rebellion by both the young and old.

People may make their own lives miserable but resist having them mess up yours.

A Father's Thoughts on Living

Be All That You Can Be

You may not be the best, but you are better than many, and you can still improve.

Do not settle for less than your best.

Good, better, best never let it rest, until your good is better and your better is best.

Walter D. Smith

If you decide to do something, do it to the best of your ability.

You may not be perfect, but at any given moment, be the best that you can be.

To be the best requires hard work and a commitment to practice.

If you expect the best from others, be prepared to give your best.

A Father's Thoughts on Living

You aren't always the best judge of what is good for you. Seek the counsel of others who have more insight, experience, and objectivity.

You may not always be the best, but always be the best you can.

Walter D. Smith

. . . and to the Republic for which it stands. One Nation under God, . . .

The United States of America is still the greatest country on earth.

Paul Harvey said, "The free are never out of debt to the brave."

Acknowledge and honor the brave at every opportunity.

A Father's Thoughts on Living

Respect and protect your country.

The price of freedom is never too high.

As an American, you need not fight to earn or enjoy your freedom; you need only to be prepared and willing to fight when it is threatened.

Family and country, like treasures, should be well guarded.

Walter D. Smith

Freedom requires vigilance and demands continuous defense to preserve it.

Some citizens viciously criticize the United States, but I haven't read lately of anyone being persecuted for trying to escape.

Show Me Don't Tell Me

Favors are granted to those who show appreciation and are willing to do the same for others.

Kind is as kind does.

One good turn deserves another.

A show of appreciation brings out the best in a person.

Walter D. Smith

Lend a Helping Hand

When you have some extra time and energy, help the needy. You will be richly rewarded.

If a person's life has been derailed, use your positive influence to help him get back on track.

Somewhere there is a cause looking for you. Keep your eyes and ears open so you can see and hear it coming.

A Father's Thoughts on Living

The valleys you conquer, the peaks you create, and the people you help are the ultimate measure of how well you have lived and used your life.

Squeeze from life all that is good and use it to help others.

Identify someone you can help, then do it.

If a person continually rejects your offers of help, move on and help another person who is more receptive.

Walter D. Smith

*You can't be all things to all people,
but be what you can.*

*Don't carry others' burdens if they aren't
willing to help themselves.*

*Use your talents and resources to help
those less fortunate.*

Time in a Bottle

*Time and money should both be budgeted,
and neither should be wasted.*

*The perception of time depends on if you are
looking forward or backward.*

*Time on a clock goes around and around.
In life, it passes only once, so use it well.*

Walter D. Smith

Time is not a renewable resource, so make the most of every minute.

Allocate time wisely. Like life, it shall not pass this way again.

The clock of life ticks continuously, and each tick is an irretrievable moment of your life.

Time is impatient and waits for no one.

Time cannot be replaced, so spend it wisely.

A Father's Thoughts on Living

*The value of time is commensurate with its use.
If wasted, it is not worth much.*

*Do something soon. It is always later
than you think.*

*Time does not go by slowly when you are having
fun or facing a deadline.*

A minute wasted is a minute lost forever.

Walter D. Smith

Twenty-four hours a day is often insufficient. Therefore, measure each task and allocate time according to its importance.

A wasted minute here and a wasted minute there soon adds up to a waste of a significant portion of your life. In a life of 80 years, one wasted hour per day adds up to nearly three and a half wasted years. Think of what could be accomplished in three and a half years.

Each minute of your life is a valuable asset, so don't waste a single one.

A Father's Thoughts on Living

In God We Trust

God has big plans for you. Accept His plan and take appropriate action.

Many are called, but few are chosen. Be ready when the "call" comes.

It's tragic to know the 23rd Psalm but not the Shepherd.
  — Anonymous

Destroying a life by murder violates the Sixth Commandment. Destruction of a life by the abuse of alcohol, drugs, tobacco, food, or any other substance or act must likewise violate one of God's laws.

Faith is the belief in the existence or righteousness of something you cannot see, feel, touch, taste, smell, or prove by the application of scientific principles.

Going to church, the synagogue, or the Mosque? Run; don't walk. God is waiting for you.

Stars, flowers, snow-capped mountains, quiet streams, and human beings are among the ways God decorated the universe. However, we were created to be more than just ornaments. Each of us has gifts to share and a Divine plan to follow.

Trust in God, but reserve judgment on others.

The Bible says, "Ask and you shall receive." It does not say that you will receive now, so be patient and continue to pray.

Walter D. Smith

Believing in God provides the comfort and strength of knowing you are never alone.

Death is only the end of mortal living. Life goes on at a new address.

Do not forget or trivialize the great gift of salvation.

Technology and tyrants may change the world and the way we live, but God is still in charge.

*Faith is strengthened by tests, trials,
and tragedies.*

*In times of need, go to Him with confidence.
Do not suffer alone or in silence.*

Walter D. Smith

Family Tradition

Like Mom said, "There's no fool like an old fool."

Your family name is precious. Treat it with respect and do not disgrace it, because you are its link between the past and the future.

Mom and Dad are smarter than you think.

Express gratitude to your mother daily.

A Father's Thoughts on Living

Don't sell moms short when it comes to protection. Like the lioness, the bear, and other mothers in the wild, a human mother will stand between her child and any threat.

Mom said, "Take care of your pennies and your dollars will take care of themselves."

Appreciate and acknowledge the sacrifices your parents make.

Walter D. Smith

Never Too Old to Learn

Know-it-alls are usually obnoxious.

Some people are poor listeners, because they think they know it all.

Many think they are right before they have stopped to think.

A Father's Thoughts on Living

Oh Happy Day

Elvis was right! Don't be cruel.

Be nice even when others are not. Your attitude, enthusiasm, and optimism are contagious.

Smiles buy a lot of friendship and goodwill.

As a fellow named Thompson said, "Be kind to everyone you meet because everyone is fighting a battle."

Walter D. Smith

Don't let someone's cantankerous nature and sour disposition spoil your good mood.

Smiles are cheap, but their purchasing power is great.

Always be pleasant.

Every day, you have many opportunities to bring sunshine into the life of another.

Keep a smile in your voice at all times, especially on the telephone.

A Father's Thoughts on Living

Every day is a beautiful day. Some are just more pleasant than others.

Every day can be a good day. It's up to you.

Shine inside and out, even when the sun doesn't.

Be real, be true, and be honest with everyone.

Smiles and laughter are messages from the heart.

Be the sunshine in someone's life today.

Walter D. Smith

The Color of Money

Having money isn't important; knowing how to spend it is. Be generous and allow others to enjoy the fruits of your labor.

If you handle your cash like a hip-shootin' Mississippi gambler, don't be surprised when you end up broke.

A Father's Thoughts on Living

Money doesn't make you better; it only makes you more fortunate.

Neither wealth nor poverty confers on you the right to be crude.

Wealth is two-faced; it can be a blessing or a curse.

A wealthy man once said, "Money is only important when you don't have it."

Walter D. Smith

Use It or Lose It

Not using one's talents is no different than not having any.

Unnurtured skills and talents will wither and die like a neglected plant.

No one was created to merely occupy space. You were blessed with special talents and have an obligation to use them well.

A Father's Thoughts on Living

Find your purpose and pursue it vigorously.

If you live with less and less purpose, your life ultimately becomes purposeless.

Blessings are gifts that are often taken for granted.

You don't have to be an athlete to be a coach.

Use your knowledge and talents to unleash the skills and abilities locked inside of others.

Walter D. Smith

The curse is not always knowing how to best use your blessings.

Time, talent, and money are valuable and limited resources.

Perform a daily inventory of your talents and blessings and use them wisely.

Your talents and blessings are not disposable, throw-away items. You have an obligation to use them in a positive manner.

A Father's Thoughts on Living

Are you maximizing the use of your greatest gifts?

Men and women were created equal and blessed with special gifts. We've merely received different gifts, and some have used theirs better than others.

Strive to use your gifts to the fullest.

The unused or under used gift should be a criminal offense.

Walter D. Smith

Many people would pay dearly for the gift you may be taking for granted.

Use your blessings in the fruitful manner for which they were intended.

All the brains, skills, and talents in the world will profit you not unless you use them.

Talent, skill, and energy, like natural resources, help no one until they are released.

*Discover your strengths and let them
lie dormant no longer.*

*Perform your stewardship well
and responsibly.*

*If you haven't discovered the meaning
and purpose of your life, keep looking.*

Walter D. Smith

Tomorrow's Leaders

Encourage children to ask questions, and respond carefully and seriously, because flippant and wrong answers can be harmful.

Remember, a child trusts you and does not always have the capacity to determine if you are kidding or telling the truth.

A child's mind is a fragile thing. Do not bruise or abuse it.

Children begin life warm, caring, loving, and trusting. Nurture those traits.

Make a difference in the life of a child.

Children should be treated as children, with love, affection, and patience.

Walter D. Smith

*If children are constantly told "you can't do this"
and "you can't do that," their natural curiosity
is subdued, their confidence becomes retarded,
and they soon believe they can't do anything.*

*Not all parents are good to, or for, their children.
Be alert for the boy or girl who can be assisted by a
positive influence or a helping hand and extend yours.*

*Each of us has the ability and capacity to be a
positive influence in the life of a child who,
without us, may grow up misguided.*

A Father's Thoughts on Living

As the Bible says, "Train up a child in the way they should go and when they are older they will not depart from it."

Spend time with your children when they are young. There's a difference between fishing with a five year old child and a twenty five year old adult.

Walter D. Smith

Love Conquers All

Love is a medicine that cures many physical and mental ailments.

Love is easy to find, inexpensive, and given graciously if you yourself are lovable.

Home should always be a refuge from the burdens and harsh realities of life.

A Father's Thoughts on Living

Puppy love is sweet, but true love is magnificent.

A loving relationship is good preventative medicine for the cares of the world that challenge you.

Love and help can only be given to a willing recipient.

Love is not nourished by threats and punishment.

A happy marriage is worth its weight in gold.

Walter D. Smith

If a man's house is to be his castle, he cannot be a one-man construction and maintenance crew. The woman of the house has the same needs. Therefore, the creation and maintenance of a cheerful, warm, safe, and loving castle are responsibilities shared by all.

Love, respect, and tranquility should begin at home.

True love has no ending.

Right and Wrong

Recognizing that an act is wrong but choosing to do it anyway is a deliberate act of defiance.

Before doing wrong, weigh the consequences and be prepared to pay the price. Right and justice will prevail in the end.

You must have enough wisdom to determine what is right and what is wrong.

Walter D. Smith

Some people may be smarter than you, but even they do not know everything and are not always right in their beliefs and understanding.

Balancing right and wrong is not a noble objective, but eliminating the wrong is a worthwhile pursuit.

Be big enough to admit when you are wrong, strong enough to defend your position when you are right, and wise enough to know the difference.

Right is easier to defend than wrong.

A Father's Thoughts on Living

Doing right is sometimes difficult.

When you are right, don't boast.

When you are wrong, graciously acknowledge and accept your error and learn from it.

Making the right choice is all the preventative action necessary to prevent bad things from happening.

Wrong has an extensive wardrobe and is clothed in many ways.

Walter D. Smith

Half Full or Half Empty?

Perception can be a great ally or a great enemy.

Look ahead with hope and promise.

Optimism is the true belief that anything that happens will ultimately turn out okay.

*Take comfort in the knowledge that the unfair
and the fair tend to balance out in the long run.*

*If you believe good things will happen, you improve
the odds dramatically.*

*Problems can be mountains or molehills.
It's a matter of how you perceive them.*

*When your burdens are getting heavy, think of all
the people who would gladly trade places with you.*

Walter D. Smith

Face each day with great confidence and optimism, because your past is forgiven, and your future is assured.

The facts of any situation will frequently change your perspective and understanding.

Things usually work out for the best.

There is truth in the old saying, "I cried because I had no shoes until I saw a man who had no feet."

A Father's Thoughts on Living

Go the Extra Mile

Mediocrity is easy.

Excellence requires focus, commitment, hard work, and persistence.

The trophy of success is not always awarded to the swift. Frequently, it is earned by the person who plods through the important, time consuming details.

Walter D. Smith

Every day is a challenge. Be prepared.

To be successful, keep on "keeping on." The less persistent will quit and narrow your competition.

When all else fails, try again and again and again. By then, the pessimists and the faint of heart will have fallen by the wayside, and the path to success will be less crowded.

If success were easy to achieve, everyone would be successful.

A Father's Thoughts on Living

Risk is one rung on the ladder of success.

A temporary fix means there is still work to be done.

Just because something is possible doesn't mean it is easy or risk free.

A project without a timetable is like a trip without a destination.

"Hard" and "Difficult" are not stop signs, but merely signals that more effort is required.

Walter D. Smith

Nothing worthwhile comes easily.

Many see the work to be done, but few step forward to do it.

Success is seldom the result of luck or an accident.

Sculpting a career or a life is like sculpting a marble statue. Both take time and patience, and you have to keep chipping away.

You can <u>soar</u> with the eagles or <u>sour</u> with the pickles and cabbage. The only difference is "u."

When you know how to measure success, it is easier to develop a program to get what you want.

A plan and a timetable are the best equipment to pave the road to success.

You can see farther from the mountain top than the valley.

You are a product of your genetics, education, experience, and environment. If you are unhappy with the present product, it is never too late to change.

Walter D. Smith

Scale the mountain and improve the range of your vision.

If you don't like what you're doing, it's time to work on your credentials.

Be of good character and effectively use your brains and talent, and you will be somebody.

If someone else can accomplish your goal, so can you.

Watch, study, learn, and take action.

A Father's Thoughts on Living

Anybody can be a nobody, and everybody can be a somebody.

Self-confidence is an important rung on the ladder of success.

The road to success is littered with failure caused by indecision and procrastination.

He thought he could not, but discovered he could.

Being a nobody is easy; just do nothing.

Walter D. Smith

Don't envy the success of others. Work hard and create your own.

You will never know how far you can go or what you can achieve until you start moving in some direction.

Preparation is half of the battle.

If you have low expectations, you will seldom be disappointed. However, you will be locked into mediocrity and miss the joy and exhilaration of stellar achievement.

A Father's Thoughts on Living

If your future is secure, day-to-day decisions become easier.

Equip yourself mentally and physically to deal with the valleys and rise to great heights.

Success is not a matter of luck. It is a matter of being prepared and recognizing opportunities.

Being a somebody requires character, vision. goals, focus, and effort.

You won't move mountains if you don't move yourself.

Walter D. Smith

Take a Chance

Maybe you can and maybe you can't, but how will you know if you never try?

Nothing ventured is nothing gained.

A Father's Thoughts on Living

When You Dream

A dream that is put on hold seldom emerges again.

Translate wishes into plans.

Wishes are hollow thoughts that require goals, objectives, and plans of action in order to produce meaningful results.

Walter D. Smith

If your wishes came true, what would you do next?

If cultivated, dreams are seeds that sprout into reality.

Keep dreaming as you steadfastly work to achieve your goals. With focus and hard work, dreams do come true.

Word Power

Words can be tools or weapons; therefore, choose them carefully and use them with discretion.

An ounce of sarcasm can kill a pound of enthusiasm.

Talk is cheap, but what you say could be costly.

Walter D. Smith

Avoid gossip.

Harsh and abusive words can create invisible emotional wounds that never heal.

Be sure of your intent before you speak.

If eyes are the windows to the soul, what is the mouth? Lately, it seems many mouths are doorways from the garbage dump. They spew forth mostly profanity and trash.

Sharp and biting words can pierce the hardest of hearts and wound the gentle one.

Always be on guard and carefully weigh the consequences of your words and deeds.

Together, sarcasm and wit may be humorous, but sarcasm alone has no redeeming qualities.

Criticism is a deadly force. It kills goodwill, motivation, and inspiration.

Walter D. Smith

Contrary to the old saying about sticks and stones, words can hurt.

A jest is often sarcasm in disguise.

The spoken word is an important factor in the impressions you create. Make sure your words are selected carefully and spoken well.

Innocent lives are often damaged by untrue or colored statements.

Unkind words and deeds are destructive weapons.

Often, remarks made in jest are not funny.

Only criticize if you end with a positive suggestion for change.

Walter D. Smith

Compassion

Injuries to the body will heal with time, but injuries to the mind and heart may never heal.

Pain is not only physical.

Do not "toy" with a person's heart and emotions.

Matters of the heart are not to be taken lightly.

A Father's Thoughts on Living

For some, grief and sorrow are eternal. Be sensitive to their needs and feelings.

Be a sedative when you can.

A broken heart bears much unseen pain.

If you really care, your actions will confirm your humanity and compassion.

Do not step on a person's toes or feelings.

Walter D. Smith

Bruised spirits and feelings heal slowly.

Hurting someone brings no pleasure.

What is good for you may be painful for someone else.

Kind and gentle is better than cruel and abrasive.

In a romantic relationship or matter of the heart, a careless word or act could cause a lifetime of grief.

Sincerity is hard to fake.

The heart speaks louder than the brain.

There is no enduring pleasure from inflicting pain or injury on others.

True concern is the door to a caring heart.

Rejection can cut deeply.

Walter D. Smith

Teamwork

The burden is lighter if it is shared by many.

No matter how good you are, you cannot do everything yourself. Create a team and revel in the success.

A secure person has no trouble sharing credit and praise.

Most significant accomplishments are attributable to a team.

The men who have walked on the moon did not get there by themselves.

Share the rewards and credit for a job well done.

Distribute the load.

Most of your greatest accomplishments will be team efforts.

Walter D. Smith

Differences of Opinion

If you must argue, argue civilly.

Anger and sarcasm are not the way to settle a dispute.

It is difficult to agree with a disagreeable person.

The cooler head prevails.

A Father's Thoughts on Living

If you are going to argue or engage in physical combat, make sure the issue deserves the effort and respect you accord it.

Few issues are worth the defense of a raised voice.

Keep your ears open, because listening determines what you say.

No one escapes unscathed from a serious dispute.

Address societal dangers and ills with harmless and socially acceptable solutions.

Walter D. Smith

Weigh each issue and determine if the benefit of being right is worth the price.

Choose your enemies carefully, because some can do you more harm than others.

A good defense is always a good offense.

Let unpleasant experiences die a peaceful and permanent death.

Anger and sarcasm generally produce more anger and sarcasm.

A Father's Thoughts on Living

Aggressive words and actions to prove you are right can damage relationships.

It's sad that we sometimes treat each other so viciously.

Don't use negative experiences as weapons in future domestic disputes.

With the unrivaled intelligence on this planet, it puzzles me that we resort to inhumanity and violence to settle our differences.

Walter D. Smith

People become ugly when they are angry.

In any conflict, the challenge is to move from the battlefield to the negotiating table.

Silence can speak volumes.

Calm, rational discussions accomplish more than arguing and fighting.

Random Thoughts to Keep You Going

Some individuals have a strong desire to bring out the worst in others.

Inspiration is a mighty force.

Smart people are not always intelligent, and intelligent people are not always smart.

Avoid negative people.

Walter D. Smith

Each household with multiple residents is a microcosm of the world as a whole.

It is possible to be alone without being lonely.

You can be strong, smart, and fast; but it means nothing unless you know where you are and what you are doing.

If a person lies about small matters, there is no assurance that he does not lie about everything.

Mirror the good in the world.

A Father's Thoughts on Living

The best way to avoid sarcasm is to stay away from sarcastic people.

Pay attention to the details.

Get all the facts before making a major decision.

Regularly express gratitude to your mentor and keep the legacy going.

With the right positive influence, people can, and do, change for the better.

Walter D. Smith

Leader of the Pack

Just because "everyone is doing it," doesn't necessarily mean that "it" is right or generally accepted.

If "everyone is doing it" is your response, you give the impression that you are a follower.

Think for yourself! Set a high standard and be the leader.

It is better to ask for help than to demand it.

To get cooperation and best efforts, smother people with sincere praise and recognition for their dedication, commitment, and performance.

If you are truly your brother's keeper, what are you doing on a daily basis for the people in your area of influence?

A successful leader takes the blame but shares the credit.

Walter D. Smith

Respect is not a right. It must be earned.

If you look down on people with contempt, do not expect them to look up to you with respect.

Don't jump on the bandwagon too quickly. It may be headed in the wrong direction.

Think for yourself and reach your own carefully considered conclusions.

A lack of self-discipline and self-control will greatly diminish your leadership role.

Effective leadership requires the ability and willingness to do what you expect of others.

Walter D. Smith

Make 'em Laugh

Laughter may not be the best medicine, but it is pretty good.

Watch for the lighter side of life.

Humor and chances to laugh are all around you.

*Music and laughter are balm for the body and soul.
Enjoy them often.*

Humor is everywhere.

*Someone said, "Laugh and the world laughs
with you. Cry and you cry alone."*

*It is okay to laugh with people, but wrong to laugh
at them unless they are clowns or comedians.*

Walter D. Smith

Lessons Learned

Even bad experiences provide useful lessons.

A mistake can be useless or a valuable learning experience.

Learn from others' mistakes as well as your own.

Experience is a great teacher.

A Father's Thoughts on Living

Misfortune need not be disastrous. It can be valuable experience for dealing with difficult situations in the future.

Experience linked with common sense and sound judgment is a powerful force.

Street smarts and common sense can be invaluable.

Even unpleasant experiences provide valuable learning opportunities.

Walter D. Smith

Challenges and tough times strengthen people like fire and heat strengthen iron.

If you could relive a bad decision, what would you do differently?

Every new experience should be a learning experience.

You can't change the past, but you can learn from it and move forward.

Bad things do happen to good people.

Even if you can't, the experience and added knowledge from trying will serve you well.

The sooner you gain knowledge and experience, the sooner you will improve the quality of the choices you make.

Walter D. Smith

False Impressions

Shy and timid individuals are often mistaken as arrogant, so don't judge too harshly or hastily.

The hearing impaired may mistakenly appear aloof by not acknowledging your greeting.

Self Control

Fun and pleasure are the spices of life. Enjoy them frequently in moderation.

Most ill-gotten and short-term gains exact a high toll in loss of jobs, family, reputation, friends, money, peace of mind, and freedom.

Winners and smiles are rare sights in casinos.

Walter D. Smith

In excess, fun and pleasure can be dangerous to your health and your wealth.

Drinking (alcohol) and driving do not mix well, nor do alcohol and countless other activities.

Enjoy a variety of experiences while maintaining balance in your life.

Life is more fun when you are in control.

Most of us succumb occasionally to evil. The challenge is to convert occasionally to rarely, or never.

Instant gratification is usually short lived.

Gambling is a one way street to the house of ruin.

Walter D. Smith

Personal Growth: Work in Progress

You grow with the challenge of providing satisfaction.

Life is pretty vanilla if you travel through it with an attitude of indifference.

If your word and handshake are your bond, it says a lot about you.

Do without before you beg.

You determine what life is and isn't, so make it something pleasant.

No matter your status, conduct yourself with dignity and show respect for others.

Change is inevitable, so adjust and move forward.

Put hard feelings behind you and move on as quickly as possible.

Walter D. Smith

What good and pleasant event has occurred in your life today? Replay it often, and it will push away the dark clouds of loneliness, fear, anger, and sorrow.

It is essential to have a reason to wake in the morning and to have something enjoyable and worthwhile to do once you are up.

Are you conservative or selfish? It is important to know the difference.

Forgive, forget, and move on with life.

A Father's Thoughts on Living

Striving for perfection leads to improvement and increased confidence.

Perfection is not only elusive, it is impossible. But that doesn't mean you should quit striving for it.

Inner strength is admirable, but it is more effective when expressed outwardly.

Do not beg for something you can obtain for yourself or something you can do without.

Walter D. Smith

Among the challenges and responsibilities of life is the obligation to live it meaningfully.

Let your deeds speak for you.

Don't think you are better than anyone; on the other hand, don't feel anyone is better than you.

Selfishness and self-centeredness have no virtue.

Contribute, because just being present doesn't mean much.

Live in a manner that leaves no regrets.

Knowing when to say "no" is as important as knowing when to say "yes."

Positive results start with positive acts.

Imitate the thoughts, words, and actions of successful people, and you can achieve similar results.

You get what you deserve; it's your job to deserve what you want.

Walter D. Smith

Be passionate about something.

Learning "not to" is often as important as learning "how to."

If you are fair and honest, you have already cleared two major hurdles between your present status and total success.

Think and act positively.

Do not quit working to improve.

A Father's Thoughts on Living

Always conduct yourself with honor and integrity.

Every individual has room for improvement.

Have a strong set of principles and the courage and strength to live by them.

It is never too late to change.

Walter D. Smith

Uncertainty

When in doubt, don't.

You are what you are, but others may not be what you think.

If a situation doesn't look right, feel right, or sound right, it may not be right. Apply healthy skepticism and suspicion and proceed with caution.

Knowledge is Power

Voracious reading is the next best thing to a formal education.

In the long run, brain power will defeat muscle power.

Keep learning and getting smarter, and you can become the expert.

Do not forget the sport of mental gymnastics.

Walter D. Smith

The mind requires frequent workouts, stimulation, and conditioning.

Thoughts are the oil that lubricates the brain. High-quality thoughts are recommended for top performance.

Reading is to the mind as exercise is to the body.

Learning must be a continuous process; otherwise, the world will pass you by.

Questions are the windows to knowledge.

A Father's Thoughts on Living

Health and Well Being

Stress is a pressure with no place to go, so find a healthy release valve and use it regularly.

Proper care and preventative maintenance of your body are recommended for a long and healthy life.

Self-destruction is easy and often subtle.

Exercise is good for you. Make it fun and extend your life.

Walter D. Smith

You're Only Human

People will forgive much misconduct if the wrongdoer is truly repentant.

Don't be afraid or reluctant to say, "I'm sorry."

You may be correct about many things, but no one is infallible.

If you are too big to say, "I'm sorry," then you are not really very big at all.

Never be too big or too self-righteous to say, "I'm sorry."

Accept and admit to human nature, because we all make mistakes.

Being kind, compassionate, and courteous may prevent you from having to say, "I'm sorry."

Walter D. Smith

Friendship

Keep networking. Friends help friends.

Be wary of strangers and give friends the benefit of the doubt.

Form as many friendships as possible, because your best friend may be the one you haven't met yet.

Be the kind of person you would choose for a friend.

*The company you keep says a lot about you.
What kind of message are you sending?*

Being alone is better than being with bad company.

*A dog may be man's best friend, but man does
not always reciprocate.*

*A true friend is one who continues to like you
during times when you are not very likeable.*

Walter D. Smith

The lone rangers often find themselves alone.

Pets, like loyal friends, deserve kindness, understanding, and affection.

Some people will do anything for you, others just say they will.

The Road to Ruin

Liars, cheats, and thieves are like weeds in a garden. Too bad there isn't a chemical to reform them.

Betraying one's trust may not be a criminal act, but it certainly is a despicable one.

Trust is an important part of character, and in its absence, there is suspicion.

Walter D. Smith

Are cheaters really winners?

Negativity is the flood that quenches the sparks of creativity, enthusiasm, and desire.

It has been said that, "War is Hell." Peace can also be Hell if there is not mutual respect and cooperation.

Suspicion fuels caution which, in the extreme, breeds paralysis in creating relationships and making decisions.

A Father's Thoughts on Living

Boasting is an attempt to promote self-importance or to elevate low self-esteem.

Fear will sap your strength.

Feelings of helplessness and hopelessness are unhealthy states of the mind and spirit.

Lying down on the job is a form of theft.

If you live life in a rut, your ambition and enthusiasm will soon be buried.

Walter D. Smith

Do not coast through life without passion.

Being rude has no redeeming qualities.

A life without faith, hope, and charity is an unfulfilled life.

Hatred seems to last forever.

If you try to bring down an honest and righteous person, you'll have your hands full.

A Father's Thoughts on Living

Poor choices lead to poor results.

Do not let hate corrupt your life.

Do not victimize yourself.

Habits are more easily started than stopped.

Suicide may solve life's problems, but it is a poor start to the Hereafter.

Misuse and abuse will eventually destroy anything.

Walter D. Smith

Desperate situations lead to acts of desperation.

Much of the unpleasantness in life is due to one's own poor choices.

Stupid acts often have tragic consequences.

The beneficiaries of selfishness are very limited.

As attractive as the benefits may seem, there are some levels to which you must not stoop.

Sinful disobedience is the garbage of life.

Give

Doing good doesn't require giving until it hurts.

The needs of the world are great. Are you doing your fair share to satisfy them?

Create ways to stay active and make contributions to the world and to your fellow travelers on the journey of life.

Walter D. Smith

Give time, talent, and money.

Loneliness is a curse that can be expelled by reaching out to give and to receive.

There is joy and pleasure in giving of your time, money, and talent.

If you can afford to give, give generously!

To make a difference, be prepared to give freely of your time, money, and self-interests.

A Father's Thoughts on Living

Lasting Impressions

Are you at peace with yourself and the people around you?

People come and go, but their influence lingers on.

Create a lasting memory by doing something of real value for someone.

Live your life in such a manner that when you die you will be missed.

Walter D. Smith

To Tell the Truth

The truth is easier to remember than a lie.

Truth is a powerful ally.

Truth and facts are easier to deal with than lies and fiction.

Truth and lies cannot coexist.

A Father's Thoughts on Living

If given the choice between smart and honest or brilliant but shady, take smart and honest every time.

Deception and lies may win a few skirmishes, but at the end of the day, the major battles will be won by honesty, integrity, and truth.

Walter D. Smith

Make the Most of It

To seize the day, jump out of bed and start running.

Today will be filled with opportunities, so take advantage of the ones that appeal to you.

Act now.

Obstacles and challenges are opportunities in disguise.

A Father's Thoughts on Living

If a meaningful task can be done in the moment, do not wait.

Be creative and resourceful.

Address a challenge as soon as possible, because it could be a golden opportunity.

Look forward to tomorrow, but do what can be done today.

Opportunities are worthless unless acted upon.

Walter D. Smith

Take Note

Memory is great, but notes are usually better.

If it's important, write it down.

Believe in Yourself

Think big and walk tall.

Henry Ford said, "If you think you can or you think you can't, you're right."

Confidence and arrogance are not the same.

Walk the talk.

Walter D. Smith

If you are not confident in yourself, who should be?

Your position may be difficult to defend, but at least you have demonstrated courage and commitment by taking a stand and articulating it.

Faith, confidence, and support will enable you to cope with life's heartbreaks, hardships, and tragedies.

Be confident enough to handle matters yourself.

Your courage and action will be rewarded.

People may curse you, condemn you, and malign you, but they will never permanently defeat you on a fair and honest field of play.

Most people face setbacks, but the strong, confident, and faithful make comebacks.

Walter D. Smith

Making Decisions and Taking Action

Often, the best course of action is no action.

An abrupt action is often ill conceived and doomed to failure. Think, evaluate, then act.

The decision to wait and see sometimes saves the day.

If You Do the Job, Do it Right!

Competency is worth nothing unless it is applied in a productive manner.

Inadequacy need not be a permanent condition.

The competent but unproductive make no greater contribution than the incompetent.

Walter D. Smith

Intelligence and experience do not always translate to competence.

One thing done extremely well is better than ten things done well enough.

It is possible to be competent but inadequate.

Forward March

Trying but failing is not a true measure of competency.

Persistence pays off.

When you are knocked down, get up.

Walter D. Smith

Staying the course in the face of unbearable odds and adversity is a sign of strong faith, courage, and confidence.

Staying the course is tougher but ultimately more rewarding than giving up.

Quitting can easily become a bad habit resulting in frequent failure and a loss of self-confidence.

Persist until you prevail.

Random Thoughts to Wrap Things Up

Influence people positively.

Face your fears head on, and you will gradually build an immunity to them.

Change for the sake of change fights for support, but positive, beneficial change gets a lot of help.

Walter D. Smith

You need not be in prison to be imprisoned.

There is a time and place for competition; home is not one of them.

Bravado is only as strong as the actions that back the words.

If death is imminent, die with dignity and honor.

Do not waste your time and resources where they are not needed, wanted, required, or appreciated.

A Father's Thoughts on Living

*It makes no sense spending your life earning a living
if you have no time to spend on your life.*

Small thoughts produce small results.

The necessities of many are luxuries for others.

Being quick and accurate is a delicate task.

*Home should be the place to escape to,
not the place to escape from.*

Walter D. Smith

Some sensitivities are senseless. Certain issues of political correctness qualify.

Some people act as if their time is gold and yours is lead.

EPILOGUE

The other morning I saw a father and his adult son working together assembling furniture. I envied them both.

Although my father had a limited formal education (8th grade), he was well read, an expert practitioner of several skilled trades, and unquestionably one of the smartest men I have ever known.

Unfortunately, he was also an alcoholic. In my youth and ignorance, I did not realize that alcoholism is a disease which

can be corrected with love and support which Dad never received. To my lasting regret, I sidestepped his attention and the opportunities to learn from him. That is why I envied the son I saw that day.

Why did I envy the father? Well, I have six wonderful children – 2 girls and 4 boys. Life is fleeting and the demands of life are often great. It seems like only yesterday that my children were born. Now, they are grown and scattered throughout the country.

There is much truth to the Harry Chapin song "The Cat's in the Cradle." In the song, the father doesn't have time for his young son. As the pace of the father's life slows down, the pace of the son's life gathers speed, and he no longer has time for his father.

Necessity often sets your priorities. It could be something as simple, and vital, as providing food and shelter for your family at the expense of their companionship.

The continuing challenge is to accept that you cannot change or relive the past, but you can take advantage of opportunities to bond and enjoy shared time in the future.

Walter D. Smith

Walt's major keynote speeches are:
"Hopes and Dreams" – Motivational and Inspirational
"Land of the Free and Home of the Brave" – Patriotic

Walt also presents standardized and customized workshops which help business owners and managers answer such questions as:

- *Is my business/department making money? (Do I really know?)*
- *Do I have adequate controls to protect the assets I manage?*
- *How can I create and implement realistic plans and monitor results to achieve my goals?*

Arrangements for keynote speeches, workshops, or consulting services can be made by contacting Walt Smith at:
102 Fourth Avenue, Baraboo, WI 53913
Phone: 608/356-7733 • Fax: 608/356-7735
waltsmith@midplains.net